New Testament Marriage

Lessons From Aquila & Priscilla

Scott ⚭ Pauley

A resource from...

First Edition, First Printing

Copyright © 2024 by Scott Pauley

All Scripture quotations are taken from the Authorized Version.
First published in 2024 by Enjoying the Journey in partnership with Faithworks Media.

Enjoying the Journey exists to evangelize the lost with the gospel of Jesus Christ, encourage pastors and local churches, and equip believers to walk with God and serve Him each day. Through audio, video, and print resources we are seeking to preach the gospel, teach the Word of God, and reach this generation for Christ.

Faithworks Media exists to provide high-quality church print resources and evangelistic material which *"adorn the doctrine of God our Saviour in all things."*

All rights reserved. No part of this book may be reproduced, stored in a retrieval system, or transmitted in any form or by any means—electronic, mechanical, photocopy, recording, or otherwise—without written permission of the publisher, except for brief quotations in printed reviews.

Layout and Cover Design by Faithworks Media
Proofing by Tammy Jones and Kimberly Wesdyk, Edited by Micah Hendry

ISBN 978-1-958301-04-3
eISBN 978-1-958301-05-0
Printed in the United States of America

"For the Furtherance of the Gospel" » faithworksmedia.com

Dedication

Tammy and I would like to dedicate this little volume to the couples who made the greatest investment in our lives and our marriage. Both of our parents have now crossed the half-century mark of marriage, and continue to demonstrate what a Christian home should look like at every season.

We lovingly dedicate these pages to:

Roger & Marcia Pauley

Bob & Chris Reis

- faithful husbands and wives, loving fathers and mothers, exemplary grandparents and great-grandparents, true Christians.

Thank you for showing us, by example, what a New Testament marriage looks like.

Foreword

" Over the years, we have become accustomed to expect Brother Pauley to give Bible truths that are theologically correct, clear, well-researched, and given with his trademark - relevant applications. This volume on marriage certainly lives up to our expectations. We anticipate that this book will bless couples because it comes from a place of sound theology and a home where Bible truth is on display.

New Testament Marriage repeatedly points out that the secret to a good marriage is not in correcting our relationship with each other, but correcting our relationship with God. In doing so, we see that improving our interpersonal relationships becomes both necessary and scripturally possible.

Aquila and Priscilla were a commendable couple, and Brother Pauley makes some observations about them that would help us all live more Christ-like in marriage: 1) As laymen, they loved God's Word and were students of it. 2) Their fervor for truth led them to encourage others to walk in it. 3) They loved Christ's Church and were active members of it.

A formula for successful marriage is given to us in the careful observation of Aquila and Priscilla. Their marriage was one that was dedicated first to God, and then to each other.

My wife and I have been married 67 years and we have learned most of what we know about marriage by trial and error. Had we been blessed with the teachings in this book, *New Testament Marriage: Lessons from Aquila and Priscilla*, we would have missed a lot of those errors.

- Dr. Charles Keen

Dr Charles Keen

Table of Contents

Introduction	Page 12
Lesson 1: Together	Page 14
Lesson 2: A Christian Home In Corinth	Page 21
Lesson 3: Open To The Word	Page 25
Lesson 4: Pass It On!	Page 30
Lesson 5: Connecting Your Family To God's Family	Page 34
Lesson 6: Your Marriage A Ministry	Page 39
Lesson 7: Faithful To The End	Page 44
Homework	Page 47
Resource: Marriages Of The Bible	Page 52
A Month Of Marriage Meditations	Page 54
Additional Resources	Page 74
Gospel	Page 78

The Story Behind The Study

If you are looking for something new in this book, you will be sorely disappointed. God's truth is not new and not old - it is eternal! We pray that in these few pages, you will gain a fresh glimpse of what God intended marriage to be from eternity past and for all of time.

Psalm 68:6 says, *"God setteth the solitary in families."* It was God who established marriage in the Garden of Eden (Genesis 1:27-28), and like every good thing that we enjoy - it was God's idea! From the beginning, the Creator designed marriage to be a relationship of spirituality, intimacy, integrity, and purity. Genesis 2:21-25 tells us,

"And the LORD God caused a deep sleep to fall upon Adam, and he slept: and he took one of his ribs, and closed up the flesh instead thereof; And the rib, which the LORD God had taken from man, made he a woman, and brought her unto the man. And Adam said, This is now bone of my bones, and flesh of my flesh: she shall be called Woman, because she was taken out of Man. Therefore shall a man leave his father and his mother, and shall cleave unto his wife: and they shall be one flesh. And they were both naked, the man and his wife, and were not ashamed."

Sin has tainted marriage horribly; it is often unrecognizable from His design. In today's culture, marriage has been minimized, corrupted, and redefined. This is why we must return to the original pattern laid out in Scripture.

Marriage is holy. It is to reflect the beautiful and powerful union of Christ and His church (Ephesians 5:22-32). The first institution ordained by God is the foundational building block of family and all of civilization. It is a revelation of what matters most to Him - and what should matter to us.

The Old and New Testaments are full of married couples who provide positive and negative examples. These husbands and wives illustrate principles that we all need. A strong marriage must be built upon Bible principles. It cannot be built upon experience, emotion, or events - all of these are changeable. Only the eternal truth of God's Word provides a foundation upon which to build.

Each couple we meet on the pages of Holy Scripture are real people with real problems. Every marriage has its stress, struggle, and strain. Social media has done much to promote the idea of "perfect" people. Filters, angles, lighting, and selective pictures only partially represent the reality of life. Many people who look like they have it all together are, in reality, coming apart at the seams. There are no perfect people, and there are no perfect marriages. **Comparison will destroy your contentment.** We all have issues to deal with, yet God has promised that as we obey His principles, He will meet every need.

What is true in one generation is true in every generation (Psalm 100:5; Ecclesiastes 1:9). While each couple is unique, each family's basic needs are the same. Those who know Christ, and have access to the Word of God, have everything they need to build a godly home (2 Peter 1:3). The institution of marriage was established in the Old Testament, and the instruction for marriage enlarges in the New Testament. The New

Testament builds on the foundation laid in the Old Testament. God's Word is a progressive revelation - it widens and deepens as it goes. New Testament Christians should desire to have a New Testament home. Those who have entered into a covenant with Christ should more deeply understand the marriage covenant.

The God of the Bible is a God of covenant. He not only makes covenants, He keeps them. Moses said, *"Know therefore that the LORD thy God, he is God, the faithful God, which keepeth covenant and mercy with them that love him and keep his commandments to a thousand generations"* (Deuteronomy 7:9).

God made covenants with Adam (Genesis 3:16-19), Noah (Genesis 9:8-17), Abraham (Genesis 12:1-3), and David (2 Samuel 7). Ultimately, He made a New Covenant that is fulfilled in Jesus Christ, the Messiah (Hebrews 9). The word "covenant" is the same as "testament." As New Testament believers, we have entered into Christ's New Covenant.

New Testament Christians should understand that God's covenants are both joyful and sobering. This is serious business! Modern marriage is often viewed as a contractual agreement, but biblical marriage is a covenant between two believers - a man and a woman - and Almighty God. In a world of broken promises, we must recognize that covenants were not made to be broken.

Christ's first miracle was performed at a wedding (John 2:1-11). He sanctified the event by His very presence and brought blessings that no one else could bring. Sadly, too many couples give attention to the wedding day and very little attention to the marriage. "Holy matrimony" is not just a sacred event; it is the lifelong pursuit of a godly home.

The Covenant of Marriage

> " I take thee to be my lawfully wedded wife, to have and to hold from this day forward, for better for worse, for richer for poorer, in sickness and in health, to love and to cherish, till death do us part.

> " I take thee to be my lawfully wedded husband, to have and to hold, from this day forward, for better for worse, for richer for poorer, in sickness and in health, to love, cherish, and obey, till death do us part.

Introduction

Our Favorite Couple

—

Tammy and I have had the privilege to teach, counsel, and work with a host of married couples. So many godly couples have impacted our marriage through the years, and we are grateful to God for those who have faithfully walked this path before us. Though they lived in another nation and another generation, the husbands and wives mentioned in God's Word provide much instruction for us. There is a reason why the Holy Spirit selected them to be in His Book.

Early in our ministry, we made a list of the couples of the Bible and what we were learning from each. (For the record, we are still learning!) It is exciting to think that we will meet all of the believing couples of the Bible someday in Heaven. But, as we meet them on the pages of Scripture, we learn so much that helps us today.

One of those couples has become very special to us. They are one of the lesser-known couples of the New Testament: Aquila and Priscilla. This husband and wife team is mentioned in four different books by both Luke and Paul. They were not church "office holders" in their day and are not world-famous today, but God used them to make a difference for eternity.

Allow us to introduce you to our favorite Bible couple…

Aquila & Priscilla

Lesson 1

⚭
Together
—

The first time we meet Aquila, and his wife Priscilla, is in Acts 18:1-3:

"After these things Paul departed from Athens, and came to Corinth; And found a certain Jew named Aquila, born in Pontus, lately come from Italy, with his wife Priscilla; (because that Claudius had commanded all Jews to depart from Rome:) and came unto them. And because he was of the same craft, he abode with them, and wrought: for by their occupation they were tentmakers."

The little word *"with"* is an important word. Even the preposition is a revelation. This is not the story of a man named Aquila or the story of a woman named Priscilla. It is the story of Aquila and Priscilla - together.

God is the One who puts husbands and wives together. However you and your spouse were brought together circumstantially, you must begin to see how God providentially worked to bring you to this moment. God gave Eve to Adam and Adam to Eve.

Marriage Math

"Therefore shall a man leave his father and his mother, and shall cleave unto his wife: and they shall be one flesh" (Genesis 2:24). The divine math of marriage: $1+1=1$. This is higher math because God's ways are higher than ours (Isaiah 55:8-9).

> *Only God can take one man and one woman and make them one, but that is His desire.*

He is the God of perfect oneness, and He alone can cause a husband and wife to be one in spirit, one in soul, and one in body (Ephesians 5:31).

When God puts people together it is always to accomplish His purpose through them and to give His best to them. This is the reason for marriage: that we can accomplish more for the good of one another and the glory of God together than we could apart.

Aquila and Priscilla were not just together in geographical location or daily labor; they were together in *all of life*. Every time they are mentioned in Scripture, they are mentioned together (Acts 18:2, 18, 26; Romans 16:3; 1 Corinthians 16:19; 2 Timothy 4:19).

When someone thinks of a husband or wife, they should also think of that person's spouse. They are not two, they are one. Matthew 19:4-6 records Jesus' words on this subject:

"And he answered and said unto them, Have ye not read, that he which made them at the beginning made them male and female, and said, For this cause shall a man leave father and mother, and shall cleave to his wife: and they twain shall be one flesh? Wherefore they are no more twain, but one flesh. What therefore God hath joined together, let not man put asunder."

The most important oneness is not physical but spiritual. For this to be true, both husband and wife must know the Lord Jesus as their personal Savior (Galatians 3:28). **True oneness is only found in Christ.** To learn more about knowing Christ as your personal Savior, take the time to read the **Enjoying The Journey** section at the end of this book. Settle your most important relationship first.

Togetherness did not mean that Aquila and Priscilla always agreed on everything. If you have been married for any length of time, you know that is impossible! Instead, it means that they were both living in agreement with God. Only as we are in step with the Lord can we stay in step with each other. The nearer we get to God individually, the closer we grow to one another in marriage.

The Foundation of Friendship

Man was created for companionship. In Genesis 2:18, we read, *"And the LORD God said, It is not good that the man should be alone; I will make him an help meet for him."* Solomon wrote in Ecclesiastes 4:9-12:

"Two are better than one; because they have a good reward for their labour. For if they fall, the one will lift up his fellow: but woe to him that is alone when he falleth; for he hath not another to help him up. Again, if two lie together, then they have heat: but how can one be warm alone? And if one prevail against him, two shall withstand him; and a threefold cord is not quickly broken."

The old king would have ended much better if he had followed his own counsel. This man had multiple wives, and lost both the intimacy of the wife of his youth, and the smile of God. Notice the wisdom that God gave him to pen - *"two are better than one."*

This is one of the greatest descriptions of true friendship in the Bible. Why is this important in marriage? Every good relationship must be built on the foundation of friendship. **Romance ebbs and flows, but friendship grows and grows.** Your greatest friendships should begin with family. Jesus taught the essentials of friendship to those He brought into the Father's family (John 15:13-15), and we must learn it too.

What a beautiful thing it is to see a real partnership in marriage! But here is the key: *"a threefold cord is not quickly broken."* We move from one person alone to two together, to a threefold cord. In the ancient world, the three-ply cord was a proverb used to suggest strength. It is not enough to have the man and the woman; we must be woven together in Christ!

The third is actually the First, the One who brings true strength to any marriage is the Lord. We need one another, and we both need Jesus. In this way, every family member is really a "dependent" - all depending on Christ.

In another one of Solomon's writings, the bride said of her groom, *"This is my beloved, and this is my friend"* (Song of Solomon 5:16). The love spoken of between the husband and wife in Song of Solomon was more than romantic emotion or sexual attraction. At its core, love is the truest form of friendship. Is your *"beloved"* also your *"friend"*?

If you are just starting into a relationship, cultivate a deep friendship first. If you cannot trust, share, and sharpen one another, then you should not be married. Your heart can deceive you because it is deceitful (Jeremiah 17:9)! Never allow emotions to overtake logic or lead your will. Do not allow changeable feelings to supersede divine confirmations or your desires to overcome good counsel.

To those who have been married for some time, continually work to deepen your friendship. Your best friend on earth should be the person with whom you have committed to spend the rest of your life. Be the friend you want. This must be worked on every day. There are varying levels of communication among friends. There is conversation, when you share what is on your mind. And then there is communion, when you share what is on your heart. The friendship of marriage should be the deepest on earth, full of heart level communication. You should be able to say, *"This is my beloved, and this is my friend."*

Sometimes a believing husband or wife must serve the Lord faithfully when their spouse is not. Keep praying, keep serving, keep believing, keep loving, and keep influencing (1 Corinthians 7:13-14; 1 Peter 3:1-6). God will say what you cannot say and accomplish what you cannot. But let all of us make our goal to develop a New Testament marriage that follows God's pattern. The Lord intends us to be *"heirs together of the grace of life"* (1 Peter 3:7).

It is not enough to simply stay married; it is the will of God that Christian couples serve the Lord together. Husband and wife are to work together to bring glory to Christ through their home. Married couples ought to pray together, read the Word of God together, attend church meetings together, and labor together to bring the lost to Christ.

Charles Spurgeon wrote concerning Aquila and Priscilla, *"When two loving hearts pull together they accomplish wonders. Here a wife and a husband are united in sincere devotion."* Nothing brings unity like a common purpose. The desire of every believing husband and wife ought to be to glorify the Lord Jesus Christ together.

Conversations About Christ

Do you ever talk with your mate about spiritual matters? It is amazing that we talk to one another about plans, finances, children, and problems - but never talk about Christ and the place He ought to occupy in our lives. True oneness requires communication. *"Can two walk together, except they be agreed?"* (Amos 3:3)

Here are a few helpful ways to set in motion a conversation about the Lord in your home:

- Tell your spouse exactly how you came to know Christ as your Savior. *"Let the redeemed of the LORD say so…"* (Psalm 107:2).

- Express to your mate how grateful to God you are for them and how much you love them. *"I thank my God upon every remembrance of you"* (Philippians 1:3).

- Share with your spouse a matter you are specifically praying about at this time. *"Bear ye one another's burdens, and so fulfill the law of Christ"* (Galatians 6:2).

- Talk with your spouse about how God has answered prayer and give Him the glory. *"O magnify the LORD with me, and let us exalt his name together"* (Psalm 34:3).

- Show your mate a truth God has recently taught you from His Word. *"For we cannot but speak the things which we have seen and heard"* (Acts 4:20).

- Explain to your spouse the spiritual goals you have in your own life. *"Not as though I had already attained, either were already perfect: but I follow after, if that I may apprehend that for which also I am apprehended of Christ Jesus"* (Philippians 3:12).

- Discuss with your mate specific opportunities your family has to minister to others. *"Look not every man on his own things, but every man also on the things of others"* (Philippians 2:4).

One fascinating footnote to the story of this Bible couple is that in four of the six references, Priscilla's name is mentioned first. This does not mean that Aquila was not the spiritual leader of the home, but it may suggest that Priscilla had a more dominant personality or was the more gifted of the two. Perhaps she was more outgoing. God makes each person and each couple unique. Husbands and wives must view each other as completers, not competitors. The right perspective is vital for marriage to thrive.

God gives the wife to the husband as *"an help meet for him"* (Genesis 2:20). He knows what each of us needs, and marriage is the place where Christian husbands and wives can become everything God has created them to be. A husband must know his wife (1 Peter 3:7), and learn to appreciate the way God made her for him. A wife must remember to respect her husband and follow him as he follows Christ (Ephesians 5:22, 33).

One thing we know is that this husband and wife operated as a team united in Christ. Aquila and Priscilla are a picture of God's ideal: a couple serving the Lord together.

> "Marriage is not a federation of two sovereign states. It is a union– domestic, social, spiritual, physical. It is a fusion of two hearts– the union of two lives– the coming together of two tributaries, which, after being joined in marriage, will flow in the same channel in the same direction…carrying the same burdens of responsibility and obligation."
> **- Peter Marshall**

Lesson 2

A Christian Home In Corinth

Corinth was one of the most wicked cities in the Roman Empire. It was known as "Little Rome." The idolatry and immorality that consumed the city was anything but the perfect environment to raise a family. Yet, Aquila and Priscilla give us a portrait of a truly Christian home in an evil place. It is possible!

If you wait until circumstances improve, or others are willing to change - you will miss your opportunity. God designed the Christian life to be lived in any situation and in every age. Christ is the One who makes having a Christian home possible - *even in Corinth*.

Christ and Your Affliction

Why were Aquila and Priscilla in Corinth? They were not on a leisure trip. They did not move there because of the appeal of the city. They had moved to Corinth because of hardship. In Acts 18:2, Scripture says Aquila had *"lately come from Italy, with his wife Priscilla; (because that Claudius had commanded all Jews to depart from Rome)…"* Even the Lord's parentheses are inspired. Don't miss the divine parenthesis in the life of this couple. **God was working in their trial to bring them closer to Himself and His purpose.**

Some things are easy to read and much harder to live. Aquila and Priscilla had lost their home and everything familiar to them. In 52 AD, all Jews were expelled from Rome. Imagine being run out of town and finding yourself in a strange and difficult place. You may be living in a parenthesis right now. Remember that no parentheses last forever, and they often give much more meaning to the story. God was at work in their affliction, and God is at work in yours.

We are not in the hands of chance or coincidence. The life of a believer is guided and guarded by Providence. When Andrew Murray was going through a period of intense suffering, he wrote in his journal: "I am here (1) by God's appointment, (2) in His keeping, (3) under His training, (4) for His time."

Our world is constantly changing, and personal circumstances will change, but Christ is always the same. *"Jesus Christ the same yesterday, and to day, and for ever"* (Hebrews 13:8). Christ can help you have a Christian home in Corinth.

Christ and Your Location

God is not bound by geography. He is not bound by anything except our unbelief! Aquila and Priscilla lived in pagan cities like Rome and Corinth, and yet they found their stability in the truth of God's Word. Their identity was in Christ. In worldly places, God connected Aquila and Priscilla to fellow Christians, granting them fuller understanding and an enlarged purpose.

Things change, but the Lord does not. His words echo through the millennia, *"I am the LORD, I change not…"* (Malachi 3:6). Remember that it was in Corinth where they would meet the Apostle Paul. Along the journey, God provides meaningful friendships with other believers. The Lord will use you to minister to them, and He will use them to minister to you. There is no doubt that Paul and Aquila and Priscilla found mutual strength from their common bond in Christ.

Several years ago, our family went through a very challenging move. In God's leading, we left a place and people that we loved very much. The first year was disorienting, in many ways, as we tried to find a new rhythm of life in a new place. Now we can look back and see that God was directing us at every step. A move that required faith and obedience became the doorway into the will of God for our whole family.

People and places change, but Christ is with you wherever you are. *"If I ascend up into heaven, thou art there: If I make my bed in hell, behold, thou art there. If I take the wings of the morning, and dwell in the uttermost parts of the sea; Even there shall thy hand lead me, and thy right hand shall hold me"* (Psalm 139:8-10). Christ can help you have a Christian home in Corinth.

Christ and Your Occupation

The Lord has an amazing way of putting people together for His own purpose. Aquila and Priscilla were tentmakers by trade, and this is the very reason they came to be so closely associated with the Apostle Paul (Acts 18:3). Imagine living and laboring with Paul every day!

There is a tendency in our thinking to divide secular and spiritual work. For the follower of Christ, all ground is holy ground, and all work is to be to the Lord (Colossians 3:23-24). My father was a bivocational pastor for many years. Like Paul and so many others, he worked two full-time jobs as a pastor and a businessman.

Work is not part of the curse. The Creator assigned it to Adam from the beginning. Work provides purpose and meaning, especially if we understand its connection to what God is doing in this world. *"For we are labourers together with God: ye are God's husbandry, ye are God's building"* (1 Corinthians 3:9).

> *Each of us have different occupations, but all of us who know Christ are part of the same work.*

There is no work like God's work! What you do for a living is not just for you; it is one component of the life the Lord has given you.

- Your work provides resources to both support your family and invest in the work of God.
- Your work provides opportunities to demonstrate the reality of Christ in the mundane and ordinary parts of life.
- Your work provides appointments with others who need to meet a true believer and hear the gospel.
- Your work provides relationships that may be essential to furthering the gospel.

You never know what God is doing through very ordinary means. Do not underestimate the occupation He has you in at this time. He may be working in ways you cannot yet see. In the words of 2 Corinthians 6:1, we are *"workers together with him."* As we connect our work to His work, we will see Him working with us (Mark 16:20).

Daily tasks sometimes change, but the larger work of Christ has not changed. He wants to use you wherever you are to serve Him and bring others to Him. Here is His promise: *"Lo, I am with you alway, even unto the end of the world. Amen"* (Matthew 28:20).

See the Lord in the details of life by looking through the lens of Scripture and the eye of faith. In a strange place during a difficult season, the all-wise God brought Aquila and Priscilla across the path of Paul. Your Heavenly Father has divine appointments, meaningful relationships, and a great purpose for you. Whatever your affliction, location, or occupation, God is at work in your life, and His timing is perfect. Christ can help you have a Christian home in Corinth.

Lesson 3

Open To The Word

Immediately after Aquila and Priscilla met Paul, we read, *"And he reasoned in the synagogue every sabbath, and persuaded the Jews and Greeks"* (Acts 18:4). Throughout Acts 18, we see Paul spending a great deal of time in this place of religious instruction helping people understand the Scriptures (Acts 18:7). Aquila and Priscilla were blessed to hear this instruction.

According to Acts 18:11, Paul spent a year and a half teaching the Scriptures in this one location, and Aquila and Priscilla were there to receive the truth. In every season of marriage, we are to be students of the Word. Husbands and wives must keep themselves under the preaching, teaching, reading, and studying of Scripture. Don't miss what God has for you!

In Acts 18:26, when another preacher began preaching, this couple was there to hear him as well. Apollos came to town, *"And he began to speak boldly in the synagogue: whom when Aquila and Priscilla had heard…"* Whenever the Scriptures were being opened, this couple was present.

Open Hearts and Open Homes

It is one thing to have an open Bible and quite another to have an open heart. Aquila and Priscilla did not have the privilege that we have to hold the completed canon of Scripture. But what an example they are of believers wide open to what God wanted to teach them!

How often do you open God's Word? Are you open to what God is trying to say to you now? This is a repeated emphasis in Scripture. God is always seeking to open the truth to us and open us to Him. The psalmist wrote in Psalm 119:18, *"Open thou mine eyes, that I may behold wondrous things out of thy law."* Again in Psalm 40:6, *"mine ears hast thou opened."* Acts 16:14 tells of a woman named Lydia, *"whose heart the Lord opened."* Satan blinds. Sin closes a man in. The Lord opens everything He touches.

An open heart goes beyond attending church meetings or listening politely when a minister gives a Bible message. Every believer must give personal attention and application of the Word of God to their own life.

Begin by keeping your own heart open to the Word. We do not start with family; we must start with our own daily walk with Christ. Spend time every day talking with God in prayer and listening for His voice as He speaks through the Word. Then, work to keep your home open to the Word. Certainly, this means that we should keep our families in a Bible preaching and teaching local church. But there is more. God doesn't just speak on Sunday; His Word works every day! Read the Bible with your family and talk about spiritual things.

> *Aquila and Priscilla's interaction with the Word was not limited to public meetings; it was woven into the fabric of their lives and daily conversation.*

The Family Altar

The term has been lost with the passing of time – and so has the use. Few people today think much about a "family altar." Yet, in days of spiritual awakening in our nation, the principle of families praying and worshiping together was vital.

The family altar does not mean that we build a physical altar in our homes. It means that we build into our schedules and routines the priority of praying with the family and talking about the Lord. The home altar is greater than the church altar in this way: it can be accessed every day.

Matthew Henry wrote, "Wherever man has a tent, God should have an altar." In the Old Testament, Abraham practiced this principle. As he moved from place to place, he erected altars to worship the Lord. In doing so, he taught his children what it meant to look to God for every need (Hebrews 11:9). Jacob learned this principle from his father (Isaac) and his grandfather (Abraham) and practiced it with his family (Genesis 35:1-7). This is a household essential in every generation.

In the New Testament, the church moved forward as prayer and the preaching of God's Word went beyond public places into every home, *"house to house"* (Acts 5:42, 20:20).

I believe in corporate worship. I believe in gathering together as an assembly (Hebrews 10:25). There is no substitute for the local church. The goal is not "house churches" (though that is necessary in some places due to persecution or pioneering work) – the goal is household worship. Every Christian family should learn what it means to pray and worship God together.

How To Begin

Norman Williams said, "The greatest Bible institute in the world is a father reading the open Bible to his family." Think of all that can be learned and taught in the home where God's Word is central, and God's Spirit is free to work!

- **Set a time and place.** Choose a time that is not hurried, when everyone can be present. You don't have to be in bondage to a time, but it will help each family member remember if it is at the same time each day.

- **Remove distractions.** Turn off all media and put mobile devices away. Quiet is a wonderful thing!

- **Make much of the Word of God.** Each person should have their own copy of the Scriptures and follow along as it is read. With little children, you have to be creative and appropriate. Use Bible stories and some sanctified imagination.

- **Talk.** This is one thing families fail to do in our busy world. Ask questions. Discuss what God is saying to each person. Deuteronomy 6:1-9 explains how the Word of God should be woven naturally into our daily interactions and conversations.

- **Pray together.** Pray for each person by name and allow each member of the family to voice their prayer to God. My pastor always said that you really don't know a person's heart until you hear them pray. Take requests and remember to emphasize the lost, the pastor and church, missionaries, and the needs of hurting people.

Where Spiritual Awakenings Start

Thomas Boston was burdened over the cold spiritual state of his church in Scotland. He began visiting the homes of his members and dealing with them specifically about their spiritual needs. He discovered that some of his people were not even sure they were saved, and many were led to Christ. In each home, he read the Bible, prayed, and challenged the head of the house to begin a family altar each day. In a matter of months, a spiritual awakening broke out in their community. It filled the church house and changed people's lives forever. It all started with a family altar.

The English Puritan, Richard Baxter, followed the same pattern in his pastorate and found the same results. When people get right with God and each other at home, the church moves forward. No one is a better Christian than the Christian they are in the privacy of their own home.

Spiritual awakenings do not begin at a church house; they begin at our house. Get open to the Word, and you will see God open His grace and truth in your marriage.

> "The woman was made of a rib out of the side of Adam; not out of his feet to be trampled upon by him, but out of his side to be equal with him, under his arm to be protected, and near his heart to be loved."
>
> **- Matthew Henry**

Lesson 4

Pass It On!

Life is a relay race. The baton of truth must not only be received, it must be relayed. Those who hear God's Word must then share it with others. This is the model God gave to ancient Israel in Deuteronomy 6 and Psalm 78. The Word moves from our ear, to our heart, to our mouth, to someone else's ear and heart! We must pass it on.

In Paul's time, one of the most exciting athletic attractions was the Isthmian Games. This parallel to our Olympic Games consisted of chariot races, boat races, boxing matches with steel-studded gloves, and a host of other events. One of the most popular competitions was the relay race. The runners had to carry a lighted torch and successfully pass it to the next runner off in the distance. This race was the source of a familiar phrase in that culture: **"Let him that has the light pass it on."**

If you have received the truth, you have the light. It is time to share it. One danger in concentrating on our marriage and family is becoming self-centered. The "my four and no more" mentality too easily creeps in. It is our privilege and responsibility to pass on the light to our own children and grandchildren, but also to many others whom God allows to cross our paths.

For Aquila and Priscilla, this included a man named Apollos. When this discerning couple heard him speak in the synagogue, they realized he had not yet been instructed in the truth Paul had taught them. This humble couple was used by God to help this brilliant orator come to a greater understanding of the gospel.

"And he began to speak boldly in the synagogue: whom when Aquila and Priscilla had heard, they took him unto them, and expounded unto him the way of God more perfectly" (Acts 18:26). There are plenty of people who want to "straighten the preacher out" but that was not their spirit. Aquila and Priscilla were used by God to simply share what they had been given. Remember that we are all stewards of the truth we have received (1 Corinthians 4:1). Truth must be guarded in our own lives but it must also be given to the next generation. Keep it and pass it on!

Apollos was a mighty preacher who was greatly used by the Lord (1 Corinthians 1:12). Yet much of his effectiveness can be attributed to the influence of Aquila and Priscilla. Imagine the good that could be accomplished for the cause of Christ if every Christian couple felt the responsibility to help others. Most believers will never have the eloquence or education of Apollos, but all of us can be used by God to encourage others.

This is always God's way. Paul told Timothy to pass on truth *"to faithful men, who shall be able to teach others also"* (2 Timothy 2:2). Titus 2 demonstrates how the older men in a church are responsible to teach the younger men, and the older women are to teach the younger women. The Apostle John said that he simply took what he had received and passed it on (1 John 1:1-5).

Many years ago, I asked my father to write a testimony of what God had done in his life and in our family. Recently, I came across what he wrote and my heart was stirred again. Permit me to share it in its entirety. As you read, consider not just what you have received but what you will leave behind...

" I grew up in a Christian home and thank God for the instruction and influence of my parents. Our family never really had much, as far as material possessions, but we were certainly blessed. My father was a preacher, and when I was a kid, Dad pastored several different churches in a short period of time. As a pastor, his monthly compensation included housing. Therefore, we lived in church parsonages for most of my young life. It seemed like a blessing at the time, but when my father died at a young age, my mother and younger brother were left with virtually nothing.

Dad was quite ill and when he died, the hospital staff returned my father's belongings. In his wallet was his driver's license, social security card, and his ordination card. There was no cash, but tucked away in a little pocket, I found three pennies. My father had no worldly possessions, this was all he had. I guess you could say - my father's "estate" was a grand total of three cents. Afterwards, I told my four siblings that I would not be dividing the inheritance. I still have those three pennies taped to a page in our family Bible. These pennies are a reminder that *"...a man's life consisteth not in the abundance of things which he possesseth"* (Luke 12:15).

As a young man, I never fully grasped the value of growing up in a Christian home with a mom and dad who truly walked with the Lord. My parents lived very modestly, but they were godly people who loved the LORD! They certainly loved each other and their five children. Even though we never had much growing up, I look back now and realize that our parents left us a wonderful inheritance! They gave each of us a legacy that is worth more than any monetary estate. Mom and Dad are both with the LORD, and one day I will see them again. Praise the Lord for the hope we have in Christ! Until that day, I am a beneficiary of my parents' faithfulness to the LORD.

"The LORD is the portion of mine inheritance and of my cup: thou maintainest my lot. The lines are fallen unto me in pleasant places; yea, I have a goodly heritage" (Psalm 16:5-6). I think often of Mom and Dad, but I also reminisce of the times I was privileged to spend with their parents. My grandparents on both sides of our family were godly people. Neither of my grandfathers were preachers, but they were faithful Christians who enjoyed serving the Lord.

God has blessed my wife and I with two wonderful children, and now six precious grandchildren. Marcia and I have enjoyed our children at every stage of their life. Even though they are now married with children, they are still our best friends. While we are enjoying the journey, we are constantly reminded of the responsibility of passing our legacy on to our children and grandchildren. It is a blessing to see both of our children serving the Lord! For many years now, it has been my prayer that God will allow me to live a life that is pleasing to Him and an example to those who follow me. Yes, I have a goodly heritage, but I must pass it on!

- Roger Pauley

The Christian home is to be a tributary of truth, a channel of blessing, pouring into the lives of others. Have you been blessed? It is so that you can be a blessing. Have you received God's comfort? Paul wrote that it is that we may *"comfort them which are in any trouble, by the comfort wherewith we ourselves are comforted of God"* (2 Corinthians 1:4). Don't keep it to yourself.

Truth is not just something we hold; it is what we are to hand off to others. Make your own list of Bible lessons that others have taught you through their instruction and example. Determine to pass it on!

Lesson 5

Connecting Your Family To God's Family

New Testament Christians love the New Testament church. It is impossible to love the Head of the church, the Lord Jesus Christ, and not love His body, the church. How important is the church? Christ loved it so much that He died for it (Ephesians 5:25). Surely those who follow Him should love the church enough to connect their lives to it!

Sadly, the priority of the church is sorely neglected among so many professing Christians. Hebrews 10:25 says, *"Not forsaking the assembling of ourselves together, as the manner of some is; but exhorting one another: and so much the more, as ye see the day approaching."* The most engaged believers ought to be the generation living on the verge of the return of Christ for His church.

Now is the time to connect your family to God's family. A New Testament church will help to strengthen the home, and a New Testament family will help to strengthen the church. These two God-ordained institutions are to work together to accomplish the divine purpose in our world.

We do not know if Aquila and Priscilla had children, but if they did, you can be sure they were impacted by the place the church held in the lives of their parents. Every time this couple is mentioned in Scripture, it is in the context of the fellowship of believers. In Acts 18, Aquila and Priscilla were a part of the church in Corinth. This same couple is addressed on the closing pages of Paul's letters to both Corinth and Rome. Notice one common expression in both references:

- *"Greet Priscilla and Aquila my helpers in Christ Jesus: Who have for my life laid down their own necks: unto whom not only I give thanks, but also all the churches of the Gentiles. Likewise greet the church that is in their house"* (Romans 16:3-5).

- *"The churches of Asia salute you. Aquila and Priscilla salute you much in the Lord, with the church that is in their house"* (1 Corinthians 16:19).

The church met in their house! In the first century, this was no small sacrifice. Followers of Christ were despised, and those who were identified with them were often marked for persecution.

Most churches did not have buildings to meet in until the third century, which meant that early believers had to find private homes in which to gather (Colossians 4:15; Philemon 2). Usually, this was the home of a family that was materially blessed enough to have a larger room to meet in. When we first met Aquila and Priscilla in Acts 18, they had been displaced and were beginning their new business in Corinth. The church met in another house. By this time, it would seem the Lord had prospered their business and allowed them to have a home large enough to host others.

It is God who gives power to get wealth (Deuteronomy 8:18), and all that we have is to be stewarded for His glory and purposes (1 Timothy 6:17-19). Because this couple was given to Christ, they had no problem giving to the Lord's work through His church. They understood that they were part of something much bigger than themselves.

More Than A Church Member

Aquila and Priscilla didn't just "go to church" - they loved the church, served the church, invested in the church, and were an active part of the church.

In a day when many do not emphasize the local church, we must connect our family to the family of God. Join your influence and the lives of those you love to a group of believers. When we belong to a local church, we place ourselves in the greatest fellowship in the world, and under accountability that every Christian needs.

The word for the church, *ekklesia,* means "a called out assembly." Here is the most basic principle for a church: an assembly must assemble! Fellowship and accountability cannot be accomplished from a distance. The first step for those who belong to a local church is to be there when the church gathers. Your presence will encourage others, build up your faith, and serve as an example for younger believers.

Once a pattern of faithful attendance is established, every believer must find their place of service in the church. Christ did not design the church for spectators but for participants. Aquila and Priscilla exercised the gift of hospitality as they opened the door of their own home to fellow believers (1 Peter 4:9-10). You don't allow the church to meet in your house if the church is not already in your heart!

The Christian home is not to be an island unto itself. God made His children to benefit from mutual encouragement and strength. The emphasis of the New Testament is not self-centered but concentrated on the needs of others.

- *"Be kindly affected **one to another** with brotherly love; in honour preferring **one another**;"* - Romans 12:10

- *"Owe no man any thing, but to love **one another**: for he that loveth another hath fulfilled the law."* - Romans 13:8

- *"Wherefore receive ye **one another**, as Christ also received us to the glory of God."* - Romans 15:7

- *"…by love serve **one another**."* - Galatians 5:13

- *"Bear ye **one another's** burdens, and so fulfil the law of Christ."* - Galatians 6:2

- *"With all lowliness and meekness, with longsuffering, forbearing **one another** in love;"* - Ephesians 4:2

- *"And be ye kind **one to another**, tenderhearted, forgiving **one another**, even as God for Christ's sake hath forgiven you."* - Ephesians 4:32

- *"Forbearing **one another**, and forgiving **one another**…even as Christ forgave you…"* - Colossians 3:13

- *"…teaching and admonishing **one another** in psalms and hymns and spiritual songs…"* - Colossians 3:16

- *"…for ye yourselves are taught of God to love **one another**."* - 1 Thessalonians 4:9

- *"Wherefore comfort **one another** with these words."* - 1 Thessalonians 4:18

- *"…edify **one another**…"* - 1 Thessalonians 5:11

- *"But exhort **one another** daily, while it is called To day…"* - Hebrews 3:13

- *"And let us consider **one another** to provoke unto love and to good works: not forsaking the assembling of ourselves together…but exhorting **one another**: and so much the more, as ye see the day approaching."* - Hebrews 10:24-25
- *"…see that ye love **one another** with a pure heart fervently:"* - 1 Peter 1:22
- *"…love **one another**…"* - 1 John 3:11, 23; 4:7, 11, 12

We should apply these *"one another"* principles first in our homes and then in the context of the church family. As we minister to one another, God will strengthen our own marriages and families.

Not everyone can fulfill the same purpose in a local assembly, but every believer has a purpose to fulfill (1 Corinthians 12). There is nothing more beautiful than seeing a family serving the Lord together, and there is not a more beautiful picture of this than Aquila and Priscilla.

New Testament Christians should build New Testament marriages and belong to New Testament churches.

Lesson 6

Your Marriage A Ministry

—

The first time we ever had the privilege of traveling in the Middle East, we visited the Dead Sea. This body of water is not just salty, it is bitter. Nothing survives at the lowest point on earth. The words of our host ring vividly in my mind: "For centuries, the Jordan River flowed into this body of water. Living things flowed constantly into it. The problem was that nothing ever flowed out of it, and life becomes death when it is kept to itself."

> *So many marriages die, not because good things do not go into them, but because nothing good ever flows out of them. Books are read, retreats are attended, sermons are heard, and lessons are learned - but life always becomes death when it is kept to itself.*

This is why people can accumulate great knowledge and experience and still be so miserable. They take in truth and blessings constantly but never learn the open secret of ministering to others.

Many couples have experienced God's goodness and heard God's truth, but they have never learned to share it. Blessed people become bitter people when they begin to think it is all about them. Many marriages have become miserable because they never had a ministry. God has designed it so that as we minister to others, it is best for them and for us! Isn't that just like our gracious God to work on both ends at the same time?

Turn your marriage inside out. Think less of what you can get out of it and more about how God can work through it to bring Him glory. Our example in all things is the lovely Son of God who *"came not to be ministered unto, but to minister"* (Matthew 20:28).

Aquila was not an apostle. Priscilla was not a pastor's wife. Yet this husband and wife affected not only their local church but also *"all the churches of the Gentiles"* (Romans 16:4). Think of the influence one couple had because they allowed God to use them. One faithful Christian couple can have a wide impact for Christ. Simple obedience sets in motion a spiritual chain reaction that far exceeds what we can accomplish ourselves.

Aquila and Priscilla ministered to the preacher in the local church.

Paul called them *"my helpers in Christ Jesus"* (Romans 16:3). Not everyone will be a leader, but everyone can be a helper. The ministry of helpers is a crucial work in every local church (1 Corinthians 12:28). Any pastor will tell you that one of the greatest needs in the church is for more workers, people who are simply willing to help. Christ's one prayer request was for more gospel laborers (Matthew 9:38). Determine by God's grace that you will be one.

It is also important to see that this service requires sacrifice. So many want to help if it is convenient. Personal comfort and public credit can never be the motivation for those who serve Christ and His church. Paul testified that this couple *"have for my life laid down their own necks"* (Romans 16:4). Are you willing to put your neck on the line?

When Paul was facing intense persecution and scrutiny, we read that he *"sailed thence into Syria, and with him Priscilla and Aquila"* (Acts 18:18). It is one thing to be "with" spiritual leadership when things are going well; it is quite another to stay with them when Satan is fighting - it requires loving commitment. At one of the hardest times in my dad's ministry, when the enemy attacked and some friends drifted away - a faithful elderly couple in our local church was used by God to greatly encourage our family. In Heaven, many of these behind-the-scenes servants will be richly rewarded for their labor of love.

We must determine that we will be givers and not just takers. Aquila and Priscilla seemed to have a special desire to help God's preachers. Two of the most effective preachers of their generation, Paul and Apollos, were both directly influenced by this godly couple.

When you minister to the minister, you have a part in all of the people to whom they will minister. By encouraging the Apostle Paul, they helped all of the churches where he ministered. The story of Aquila and Priscilla is the story of influence, influence yielded to God and used for His glory. Pray for the preacher, and speak a word of encouragement to him. The whole church will be better because of it.

Aquila and Priscilla ministered to the people in the local church.

When Paul was closing his first letter to the church at Corinth, he wrote, *"Aquila and Priscilla salute you much in the Lord"* (1 Corinthians 16:19). Following the letters of Paul, we discover that this couple moved from Rome to Corinth, from Corinth to Ephesus, from Ephesus back to Rome, and finally back to Ephesus. How wonderful to see that wherever they lived, they connected their lives and families to God's work in a local church. When Paul wrote to Corinth, they were living in Ephesus and sent a special greeting to fellow believers back in Corinth. By the time he wrote to the church in Rome, they already had the church meeting in their house (Romans 16:3-5). They were encouragers!

Ask the Lord to make you an Aquila and Priscilla in your church. Speak kind words and seek to be a blessing to as many people as possible. Your family needs the local church and your local church needs your family.

- Pray for God's blessing on your pastor and his family every day.

- Invite a family into your home for a meal and Christian fellowship.

- Write your pastor and his wife a note of encouragement.

- Visit another couple that is experiencing trouble and pray with them.

- Call someone who has made a great difference in your life, and let them know that you are grateful to God for them.

- Befriend an unsaved or unchurched couple, and seek to reach them for Christ.

- Attend the services of your local church faithfully, and encourage others to do the same.

- Pay the tithe and give offerings through your local assembly.

- Engage in gospel outreach with other believers.

- Teach another younger couple truths from God's Word which have been a great help to you and your family.

- Think of specific ways to involve your children in the local church.

- Seek to build up others as you speak to them. Avoid the temptation to be critical and negative in your conversations.

You may not be able to do everything, but you can do something. And you can lead your family to do the same. Begin right where you are, and begin in your own home. *"As for me and my house, we will serve the LORD"* (Joshua 24:15).

> *"There is no more lovely, friendly and charming relationship, communion or company than a good marriage."*
>
> *"Let the wife make the husband glad to come home, and let him make her sorry to see him leave."*
>
> **- Martin Luther**

Lesson 7

Faithful To The End

People remember how you start and how you finish - how you come and how you go. Many couples start strong, and stay strong for a season, but fail to finish well. Young couples give much attention to their first home and early years. How much consideration have we given to the final years?

You don't decide when you get to the end how you want to finish; you are choosing that every day. The last mention of Aquila and Priscilla in Scripture leaves a lasting lesson for us all. In the closing of Paul's final letter to Timothy, we find this simple expression: *"Salute Prisca and Aquila"* (2 Timothy 4:19).

This is more than a mere formality or nicety. Nothing in the Word of God is there by accident. It would appear that this couple is now back in Ephesus, helping another young preacher in the work of God. Some have surmised that they were forced to leave Rome again because of Nero's persecution of Christians. In every season of life, there are trials, and there are opportunities.

Clarence Sexton used to say that the prime of life is any time in life when you are in the center of God's will. You never know the time or place when God will use you to make your greatest contribution to the cause of Christ, but if you are breathing, it is evidence He has not yet finished with you. In every trial, realize that there is an opportunity to be used by God. Don't quit before God is finished!

In the end, perhaps the best description of Aquila and Priscilla, and the greatest thing that could be said of any believer, is that they were faithful. More than 15 years have passed since Paul first met Aquila and Priscilla, and they are still faithful to one another, faithful to Christ, and faithful to the church.

Little is known of their talents and abilities. Nothing is known of their business accomplishments or worldly goods. One thing is known of this New Testament couple - the only thing that matters - they were faithful.

- Proverbs 20:6 observes, *"Most men will proclaim every one his own goodness: but a faithful man who can find?"*
- 1 Corinthians 4:2 declares, *"Moreover it is required in stewards, that a man be found faithful."*

This should be the prayer and passion of every godly man and woman: to be faithful to their Savior, their spouse, and their God-given assignments, faithful to the end. It is fascinating that 2,000 years later, we are still talking about the contribution this couple made to the cause of Christ. They are still being used! How would you like to be remembered?

A Stark Contrast

There is a stark contrast to Aquila and Priscilla in the book of Acts as well. In chapter five we read the tragic story of Ananias and Sapphira. This couple had every opportunity and blessing that a Christian family could have. They were members of the first church in Jerusalem!

The story of Ananias and Sapphira is marred by lies and deceit, while Aquila and Priscilla loved and lived the truth.

Acts 5:2-3 says that Ananias and Sapphira *"kept back part."* Aquila and Priscilla kept back nothing! All was given to God.

Ananias and Sapphira *"agreed together to tempt the Spirit of the Lord"* (Acts 5:9). Aquila and Priscilla had agreed together to follow the Spirit of the Lord. The world is full of couples like Ananias and Sapphira, but the church should be full of couples like Aquila and Priscilla.

A study of the life of Ananias and Sapphira brings holy fear - the fear of sin and the fear of God (Acts 5:11). But a study of the life of Aquila and Priscilla brings gratitude. Paul said, *"…unto whom not only I give thanks, but also all the churches of the Gentiles"* (Romans 16:4). We, too, are thankful for how God has used this couple to influence our lives and marriage.

Aquila and Priscilla lived in the challenging early days of the church age. In God's providence, we have been chosen to live near the end of the age, just before the return of Christ. *"This know also, that in the last days perilous times shall come"* (2 Timothy 3:1). This husband and wife are a continuing reminder that you can have a New Testament marriage even in perilous times.

Our Homework

Use these pages to write down truth God is teaching you from His Word and the next steps to take in your own walk with Christ and your spouse.

Resource

Marriages Of The Bible

"Now all these things happened unto them for ensamples: and they are written for our admonition, upon whom the ends of the world are come" (1 Corinthians 10:11).

Build your marriage on Bible principles. Take the following representative couples as a starter list for further study. Read the Scriptures and discuss the positive and negative examples found in each home.

- **Adam and Eve:** Genesis 2:18-25, 4:1 — the principle of oneness
- **Noah and his wife:** Genesis 6:6-11, 7:1-16; Hebrews 11:7 — the principle of obedience
- **Abraham and Sarah:** Genesis 12:1-5 — the principle of submission
- **Lot and his wife:** Genesis 13:10-13, 19:1-38; Luke 17:32 — the principle of separation
- **Isaac and Rebekah:** Genesis 24:62-67 — the principle of love
- **Jacob and Rachel:** Genesis 29:18-20, 35:19-20 — the principle of life
- **Joseph and Asenath:** Genesis 41:45-52 — the principle of fruitfulness

- **Amram and Jochebed:** Exodus 2:1-10; Hebrews 11:23 — the principle of courage

- **Moses and Zipporah:** Exodus 4:19-26 — the principle of initiative

- **Othniel and Achsah:** Joshua 15:16-19; Judges 1:11-26, 3:7-11 — the principle of diligence

- **Boaz and Ruth:** Ruth 4:10-13, 18-22 — the principle of heritage

- **Elkanah and Hannah:** 1 Samuel 1:1-28 — the principle of prayer

- **Nabal and Abigail:** 1 Samuel 25 — the principle of discernment

- **David and Michal:** 2 Samuel 6:12-23 — the principle of worship

- **Ahab and Jezebel:** 1 Kings 16:33, 21:25 — the principle of rebellion

- **Job and his wife:** Job 2:9-10 — the principle of influence

- **Solomon and the Shulamite:** Song of Solomon — the principle of intimacy

- **Hosea and Gomer:** Hosea 3, 14 — the principle of forgiveness

- **Joseph and Mary:** Matthew 1; Luke 2 — the principle of faith

- **Zacharias and Elisabeth:** Luke 1 — the principle of patience

- **Cleopas and his wife:** John 19:25; Luke 24:13-35 — the principle of encouragement

- **Ananias and Sapphira:** Acts 5:1-11 — the principle of truthfulness

- **Aquila and Priscilla:** Acts 18:2, 18, 26; Romans 16:3; 1 Corinthians 16:19; 2 Timothy 4:19 — the principle of partnership

- **Philemon and Apphia:** Philemon 1-7 — the principle of service

- **Christ and His Church:** Ephesians 5:25-32; Revelation 19:7-9 — the principle of perfection

Resource

A Month Of Marriage Meditations

—

"This book of the law shall not depart out of thy mouth; but thou shalt meditate therein day and night, that thou mayest observe to do according to all that is written therein: for then thou shalt make thy way prosperous, and then thou shalt have good success" (Joshua 1:8).

Scripture is the great marriage manual. The following passages have been selected for husbands and wives to reflect on and discuss. Bring God's Word into your marriage and you will bring God's blessing upon your home. How can God's truth be applied to your marriage?

Day 1

Genesis 1:27-28
So God created man in his own image, in the image of God created he him; male and female created he them. And God blessed them, and God said unto them, Be fruitful, and multiply, and replenish the earth,

and subdue it: and have dominion over the fish of the sea, and over the fowl of the air, and over every living thing that moveth upon the earth.

___

Day 2

Genesis 2:18, 21-25
And the LORD God said, It is not good that the man should be alone; I will make him an help meet for him…And the LORD God caused a deep sleep to fall upon Adam, and he slept: and he took one of his ribs, and closed up the flesh instead thereof; And the rib, which the LORD God had taken from man, made he a woman, and brought her unto the man. And Adam said, This is now bone of my bones, and flesh of my flesh: she shall be called Woman, because she was taken out of Man. Therefore shall a man leave his father and his mother, and shall cleave unto his wife: and they shall be one flesh. And they were both naked, the man and his wife, and were not ashamed.

Day 3

Deuteronomy 6:4-9

Hear, O Israel: The LORD our God is one LORD: And thou shalt love the LORD thy God with all thine heart, and with all thy soul, and with all thy might. And these words, which I command thee this day, shall be in thine heart: And thou shalt teach them diligently unto thy children, and shalt talk of them when thou sittest in thine house, and when thou walkest by the way, and when thou liest down, and when thou risest up. And thou shalt bind them for a sign upon thine hand, and they shall be as frontlets between thine eyes. And thou shalt write them upon the posts of thy house, and on thy gates.

Day 4

Joshua 24:15

And if it seem evil unto you to serve the LORD, choose you this day whom ye will serve; whether the gods which your fathers served that were on the other side of the flood, or the gods of the Amorites, in whose land ye dwell: but as for me and my house, we will serve the LORD.

Day 5

Psalms 127-128

Except the LORD build the house, they labour in vain that build it: except the LORD keep the city, the watchman waketh but in vain. It is vain for you to rise up early, to sit up late, to eat the bread of sorrows: for so he giveth his beloved sleep. Lo, children are an heritage of the LORD: and the fruit of the womb is his reward. As arrows are in the hand of a mighty man; so are children of the youth. Happy is the man that hath his quiver full of them: they shall not be ashamed, but they shall speak with the enemies in the gate.

Blessed is every one that feareth the LORD; that walketh in his ways. For thou shalt eat the labour of thine hands: happy shalt thou be, and it shall be well with thee. Thy wife shall be as a fruitful vine by the sides of thine house: thy children like olive plants round about thy table. Behold, that thus shall the man be blessed that feareth the LORD. The LORD shall bless thee out of Zion: and thou shalt see the good of Jerusalem all the days of thy life. Yea, thou shalt see thy children's children, and peace upon Israel.

Day 6

Proverbs 5:15-21

Drink waters out of thine own cistern, and running waters out of thine own well. Let thy fountains be dispersed abroad, and rivers of waters in the streets. Let them be only thine own, and not strangers' with thee. Let thy fountain be blessed: and rejoice with the wife of thy youth. Let her be as the loving hind and pleasant roe; let her breasts satisfy thee at all times; and be thou ravished always with her love. And why wilt thou, my son, be ravished with a strange woman, and embrace the bosom of a stranger? For the ways of man are before the eyes of the LORD, and he pondereth all his goings.

Day 7

Proverbs 18:22

Whoso findeth a wife findeth a good thing, and obtaineth favour of the LORD.

Day 8

Proverbs 19:13-14

A foolish son is the calamity of his father: and the contentions of a wife are a continual dropping. House and riches are the inheritance of fathers: and a prudent wife is from the LORD.

Day 9

Proverbs 21:9, 19

It is better to dwell in a corner of the housetop, than with a brawling woman in a wide house…It is better to dwell in the wilderness, than with a contentious and an angry woman.

Day 10

Proverbs 31:10-12, 28-31

Who can find a virtuous woman? for her price is far above rubies. The heart of her husband doth safely trust in her, so that he shall have no need of spoil. She will do him good and not evil all the days of her life…Her children arise up, and call her blessed; her husband also, and he praiseth her. Many daughters have done virtuously, but thou excellest them all. Favour is deceitful, and beauty is vain: but a woman that feareth the LORD, she shall be praised. Give her of the fruit of her hands; and let her own works praise her in the gates.

Day 11

Ecclesiastes 4:9-12

Two are better than one; because they have a good reward for their labour. For if they fall, the one will lift up his fellow: but woe to him that is alone when he falleth; for he hath not another to help him up. Again, if two lie together, then they have heat: but how can one be warm alone? And if one prevail against him, two shall withstand him; and a threefold cord is not quickly broken.

Day 12

Song of Solomon 5:16b; 6:3a
This is my beloved, and this is my friend, O daughters of Jerusalem…I am my beloved's, and my beloved is mine…

Day 13

Matthew 19:4-6
And he answered and said unto them, Have ye not read, that he which made them at the beginning made them male and female, And said,

For this cause shall a man leave father and mother, and shall cleave to his wife: and they twain shall be one flesh? Wherefore they are no more twain, but one flesh. What therefore God hath joined together, let not man put asunder.

Day 14

John 15:12-13
This is my commandment, That ye love one another, as I have loved you. Greater love hath no man than this, that a man lay down his life for his friends.

Day 15

Romans 12:9-13
Let love be without dissimulation. Abhor that which is evil; cleave to

that which is good. Be kindly affectioned one to another with brotherly love; in honour preferring one another; Not slothful in business; fervent in spirit; serving the Lord; Rejoicing in hope; patient in tribulation; continuing instant in prayer; Distributing to the necessity of saints; given to hospitality.

Day 16

Romans 13:9-10

For this, Thou shalt not commit adultery, Thou shalt not kill, Thou shalt not steal, Thou shalt not bear false witness, Thou shalt not covet; and if there be any other commandment, it is briefly comprehended in this saying, namely, Thou shalt love thy neighbour as thyself. Love worketh no ill to his neighbour: therefore love is the fulfilling of the law.

Day

1 Corinthians 7:2-5

Nevertheless, to avoid fornication, let every man have his own wife, and let every woman have her own husband. Let the husband render unto the wife due benevolence: and likewise also the wife unto the husband. The wife hath not power of her own body, but the husband: and likewise also the husband hath not power of his own body, but the wife. Defraud ye not one the other, except it be with consent for a time, that ye may give yourselves to fasting and prayer; and come together again, that Satan tempt you not for your incontinency.

_____

_____

_____

_____

_____

Day 18

1 Corinthians 13:4-7

Charity suffereth long, and is kind; charity envieth not; charity vaunteth not itself, is not puffed up, Doth not behave itself unseemly, seeketh not her own, is not easily provoked, thinketh no evil; Rejoiceth not in iniquity, but rejoiceth in the truth; Beareth all things, believeth all things, hopeth all things, endureth all things.

_____

_____

Day 19

1 Corinthians 16:13-14

Watch ye, stand fast in the faith, quit you like men, be strong. Let all your things be done with charity.

Day 20

Galatians 5:13-15

For, brethren, ye have been called unto liberty; only use not liberty for an occasion to the flesh, but by love serve one another. For all the law is fulfilled in one word, even in this; Thou shalt love thy neighbour as thyself. But if ye bite and devour one another, take heed that ye be not consumed one of another.

Day 21

Ephesians 4:25-32

Wherefore putting away lying, speak every man truth with his neighbour: for we are members one of another. Be ye angry, and sin not: let not the sun go down upon your wrath: Neither give place to the devil. Let him that stole steal no more: but rather let him labour, working with his hands the thing which is good, that he may have to give to him that needeth. Let no corrupt communication proceed out of your mouth, but that which is good to the use of edifying, that it may minister grace unto the hearers. And grieve not the holy Spirit of God, whereby ye are sealed unto the day of redemption. Let all bitterness, and wrath, and anger, and clamour, and evil speaking, be put away from you, with all malice: And be ye kind one to another, tenderhearted, forgiving one another, even as God for Christ's sake hath forgiven you.

_____

_____

_____

_____

_____

Day 22

Ephesians 5:1-4

Be ye therefore followers of God, as dear children; And walk in love, as Christ also hath loved us, and hath given himself for us an offering and a sacrifice to God for a sweetsmelling savour. But fornication, and all uncleanness, or covetousness, let it not be once named among you, as becometh saints; Neither filthiness, nor foolish talking, nor jesting, which are not convenient: but rather giving of thanks.

Day 23

Ephesians 5:22-33

Wives, submit yourselves unto your own husbands, as unto the Lord. For the husband is the head of the wife, even as Christ is the head of the church: and he is the saviour of the body. Therefore as the church is subject unto Christ, so let the wives be to their own husbands in every thing. Husbands, love your wives, even as Christ also loved the church, and gave himself for it; That he might sanctify and cleanse it with the washing of water by the word, That he might present it to himself a glorious church, not having spot, or wrinkle, or any such thing; but that it should be holy and without blemish. So ought men to love their wives as their own bodies. He that loveth his wife loveth himself. For no man ever yet hated his own flesh; but nourisheth and cherisheth it, even as the Lord the church: For we are members of his body, of his flesh, and of his bones. For this cause shall a man leave his father and mother, and shall be joined unto his wife, and they two shall be one flesh. This is a great mystery: but I speak concerning Christ and the church. Nevertheless let every one of you in particular so love his wife even as himself; and the wife see that she reverence her husband.

Day 24

Ephesians 6:1-4

Children, obey your parents in the Lord: for this is right. Honour thy father and mother; (which is the first commandment with promise;) That it may be well with thee, and thou mayest live long on the earth. And, ye fathers, provoke not your children to wrath: but bring them up in the nurture and admonition of the Lord.

Day 25

Philippians 2:1-5

If there be therefore any consolation in Christ, if any comfort of love, if any fellowship of the Spirit, if any bowels and mercies, Fulfil ye my joy, that ye be likeminded, having the same love, being of one accord, of one mind. Let nothing be done through strife or vainglory; but in lowliness of mind let each esteem other better than themselves. Look not every man on his own things, but every man also on the things of others. Let this mind be in you, which was also in Christ Jesus.

Day 26

Colossians 3:12-21

Put on therefore, as the elect of God, holy and beloved, bowels of mercies, kindness, humbleness of mind, meekness, longsuffering; Forbearing one another, and forgiving one another, if any man have a quarrel against any: even as Christ forgave you, so also do ye. And above all these things put on charity, which is the bond of perfectness. And let the peace of God rule in your hearts, to the which also ye are called in one body; and be ye thankful. Let the word of Christ dwell in you richly in all wisdom; teaching and admonishing one another in psalms and hymns and spiritual songs, singing with grace in your hearts to the Lord. And whatsoever ye do in word or deed, do all in the name of the Lord Jesus, giving thanks to God and the Father by him. Wives, submit yourselves unto your own husbands, as it is fit in the Lord. Husbands, love your wives, and be not bitter against them. Children, obey your parents in all things: for this is well pleasing unto the Lord. Fathers, provoke not your children to anger, lest they be discouraged.

Day 27

Titus 2:1-6
But speak thou the things which become sound doctrine: That the aged men be sober, grave, temperate, sound in faith, in charity, in patience. The aged women likewise, that they be in behaviour as becometh holiness, not false accusers, not given to much wine, teachers of good things; That they may teach the young women to be sober, to love their husbands, to love their children, To be discreet, chaste, keepers at home, good, obedient to their own husbands, that the word of God be not blasphemed. Young men likewise exhort to be sober minded.

Day 28

Hebrews 13:4
Marriage is honourable in all, and the bed undefiled: but

whoremongers and adulterers God will judge. Let your conversation be without covetousness; and be content with such things as ye have: for he hath said, I will never leave thee, nor forsake thee.

Day 29

1 Peter 3:1-7

Likewise, ye wives, be in subjection to your own husbands; that, if any obey not the word, they also may without the word be won by the conversation of the wives; While they behold your chaste conversation coupled with fear. Whose adorning let it not be that outward adorning of plaiting the hair, and of wearing of gold, or of putting on of apparel; But let it be the hidden man of the heart, in that which is not corruptible, even the ornament of a meek and quiet spirit, which is in the sight of God of great price. For after this manner in the old time the holy women also, who trusted in God, adorned themselves, being in subjection unto their own husbands: Even as Sara obeyed Abraham, calling him lord: whose daughters ye are, as long as ye do well, and are not afraid with any amazement. Likewise, ye husbands, dwell with them according to knowledge, giving honour unto the wife, as unto the weaker vessel, and as being heirs together of the grace of life; that your prayers be not hindered.

Day 30

1 Peter 3:8-12

Finally, be ye all of one mind, having compassion one of another, love as brethren, be pitiful, be courteous: Not rendering evil for evil, or railing for railing: but contrariwise blessing; knowing that ye are thereunto called, that ye should inherit a blessing. For he that will love life, and see good days, let him refrain his tongue from evil, and his lips that they speak no guile: Let him eschew evil, and do good; let him seek peace, and ensue it. For the eyes of the Lord are over the righteous, and his ears are open unto their prayers: but the face of the Lord is against them that do evil.

Day 31

1 John 4:7-8

Beloved, let us love one another: for love is of God; and every one that loveth is born of God, and knoweth God. He that loveth not knoweth not God; for God is love.

_____

_____

_____

_____

_____

> *"Marriage is a call to die to self...Christian marriage vows are the inception of a lifelong practice of death, of giving over not only all you have, but all you are. Is this a grim gallows call? Not at all! It is no more grim than dying to self and following Christ. In fact, those who lovingly die for their [spouses] are those who know the most joy, have the most fulfilling marriages, and experience the most love."*
>
> **- R. Kent Hughes**

Additional Resources

—

"...when thou comest, bring with thee...the books, but especially the parchments" (2 Timothy 4:13).

The following resources will be beneficial for further study on a variety of issues related to marriage and family. This list of recommendations is not exhaustive or a total endorsement. However, these are helpful tools as we work to build stronger homes.

Marriage

- *Are We There Yet?* by Paul and Terrie Chappell
- *Cherish* by Gary Thomas
- *Love Life for Every Married Couple* by Ed Wheat
- *Love and Respect* by Emerson Eggerichs
- *Making Your Marriage a Fortress* by Gary Thomas
- *Point Man* by Steve Ferrar
- *Sacred Marriage* by Gary Thomas
- *The Five Love Languages: The Secret to Love That Lasts* by Gary Chapman
- *The Marriage Ring* by Michael and Amy Edwards

The Christian Home

- *Already Gone* by Ken Ham and Britt Beemer
- *Christian Living in the Home* by Jay Adams
- *How To Raise Your Children for Christ* by Andrew Murray
- *King Me - What Every Son Wants and Needs From His Father* by Steve Farrar
- *Making Home Work* by Paul Chappell
- *Shepherding a Child's Heart* by Ted Tripp
- *The Christian Home* by Clarence Sexton
- *Will They Stand: Parenting Kids to Face the Giants* by Ken Ham
- *Expressions of Love* by Clarence Sexton

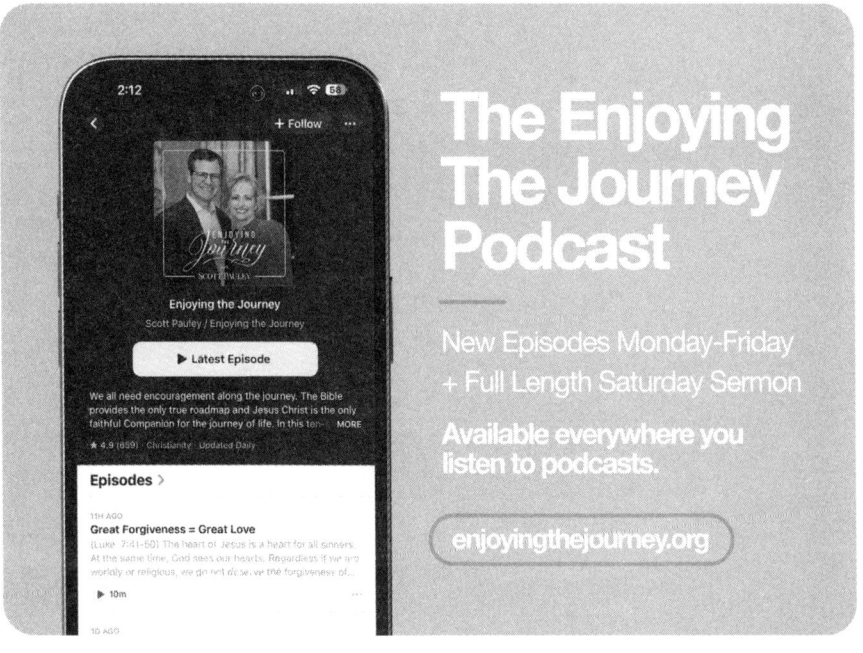

On Purpose
By Stacie Thomas

ON PURPOSE was written by Stacie Thomas, a mother, long time children's worker, and elementary school teacher. This beautifully illustrated book teaches the truth of Creation, identity, and divine purpose for every boy and girl. This resource, the first in a series of Little Steps books from Enjoying the Journey, will be a wonderful tool for parents to use with toddlers and teachers to use in both school and church settings.

The Lord Was With Joseph

By Scott Pauley

Study Guide Available

Discover the one secret to the blessing of God at every stage in life. From youth to old age, through blessings and burdens, Joseph's life is a lesson in how to live consciously in the presence of God.

Revival Praying

By Scott Pauley

Study Guide Available

Is revival possible in our generation? Revival cannot be manufactured or manipulated. Spiritual awakenings come when God's people connect their prayers to God's purpose. In Revival Praying you will discover how one of the great prayers of the Bible can serve as a pattern for our prayer.

Gospel

Enjoying The Journey

Life is a short trip to somewhere forever! How will you make the trip?

We live in a mobile society and it seems that everyone is in a hurry to get where they are going! Life itself is a journey and all of us are headed somewhere forever. An all-wise God has designed it so that those who follow His way can enjoy Heaven someday and also enjoy the journey today. The Bible, God's Word to man, is the roadmap for time and eternity.

Begin by determining your destination.

Every journey begins by settling where you are going. Without direction, we all just wander aimlessly through life, searching for meaning and purpose. Thousands of years ago a prophet named Isaiah wrote, *"All we like sheep have gone astray; we have turned every one to his own way; and the Lord hath laid on him the iniquity of us all."* [1] Some things never change!

---

1 Isaiah 53:6

"For all have sinned and come short of the glory of God." [2] On our own we all go away from God. This is why Jesus Christ came: to take our sin and give us His salvation. Only He can return us to the path we were created to walk and bring us to God. Jesus said, *"I am the way, the truth, and the life: no man cometh unto the Father, but by me."* [3]

Jesus Christ died for our sins, rose from the dead to offer us eternal life, and stands ready now to forgive our sins. But each of us must choose for ourselves if we will follow our way or His. When Jesus was on earth He said, *"Enter ye in at the strait gate: for wide is the gate, and broad is the way, that leadeth to destruction, and many there be which go in thereat: Because strait is the gate, and narrow is the way, which leadeth unto life, and few there be that find it."* [4]

There are only two destinations: eternity in Heaven with God or separated from God forever in Hell. All roads cannot lead to the same place. Our way leads us from God; Christ's way leads us to God. If you continue on the path you are on now, where will you spend eternity? You must determine your destination.

Discover the companionship of Christ.

The journey is always better with a companion, someone with whom we share both the joys and trials of the trip. This is why Jesus Christ came to this earth. He traveled this same road for thirty-three years. The Son of God is not a person far away who, *"cannot be touched with the feeling of our infirmities; but was in all points tempted like as we are, yet without sin."* [5] He knows where you are and what you are facing!

Even more, He wants to make the journey with you right now. This personal relationship begins at the moment that you place your faith in

---

2   Romans 3:23
3   John 14:6
4   Matthew 7:13-14
5   Hebrews 4:15

Him and call on Him to be your Savior. *"That if thou shalt confess with thy mouth the Lord Jesus, and shalt believe in thine heart that God hath raised him from the dead, thou shalt be saved."* [6]

When a person comes to know Christ, two things are made sure: they will live with Christ forever in Heaven, and Christ comes to live in their heart now! In one of the most famous psalms, Psalm 23, David explains it this way, *"Surely goodness and mercy shall follow me all the days of my life: and I will dwell in the house of the Lord for ever."* [7]

To follow Christ is to have Him make the journey with you, never alone! In some of His last words to the first disciples He said, *"...I am with you alway, even unto the end of the world. Amen."* [8] There will be difficulties along the way, but He will guard us and guide us at every step.

Know what to do at important intersections.

Intersections are turning points. At each of them there is a decision to be made. Life is full of decisions, but the most important ones are the ones that affect eternity. Today you are standing at one of those crossroads. You will either choose to follow Christ or to continue on your own way. Remember that a wrong turn doesn't lead to the right place! The right turn is to repent and believe on Christ.[9]

There are two paths and we all must decide which one we will take. Jesus said, *"He that believeth on him is not condemned: but he that believeth not is condemned already, because he hath not believed in the name of the only begotten Son of God."* [10] Will you believe on Christ today?

6 Romans 10:9
7 Psalm 23:6
8 Matthew 28:20
9 Acts 20:21
10 John 3:18

Call on Him now! "Dear God, be merciful to me a sinner. I know that you died for me and believe that you rose from the dead. Please forgive my sin and come into my life. I trust you now as my personal Savior. Thank you for giving me the free gift of eternal life. In Jesus' name, Amen."

This is the beginning of your journey with Jesus. He promises those who belong to Him, *"I will never leave thee, nor forsake thee."*[11] We would love to hear from you and help you as you begin to walk with Christ.

Visit us at **enjoyingthejourney.org** to take the next step.

11 Hebrews 13:5

Want To Know More?

Following God's Word & Finding Christ's Joy